Prisms of Life

By

Dr. Roopinder Dogra

Gullybaba Publishing House Pvt. Ltd

GULLYBABA PUBLISHING HOUSE PVT. LTD.

ISO 9001 & ISO 14001 CERTIFIED CO.

Regd. Office: 2525/193, 1st Floor, Onkar Nagar-A, Tri Nagar, Delhi-110035, (From Kanhaiya Nagar Metro Station Towards Old Bus Stand)

Branch Office: 1A/2A, 20, Hari Sadan, Ansari Road, Daryaganj, New Delhi-110002

Ph.: 09350849407, 011-27387998

E-mail: hello@gullybaba.com

Websites: GullyBaba.com, Gullybabakids.com

First Edition: 2019

ISBN: 978-93-88149-70-9

Copyright© 2019, Publisher

Prisms of Life

Too Close To Disclose

I don't mention any particular dates, years, names of any cities or countries for the sake of confidentiality.

Many devastating facts are not disclosed on grounds of humanity.

Efforts have been made not to hurt anyone's sentiments personally.

Writing this, led me to many emotional breakdowns time and again...

Preface

Fiction of how blood turns white and how the world dances to the tunes of money, lust, infidelity and dacoity...

'Where do I stand,

I'm a MISFIT

That's all I can understand'...

Gratitude

My parents' everlasting love and immortal memories kept me going, coming every night into my dreams, saying to MOVE ON...

YOU instigated this long buried, forgotten thought into me being my constant hope, my constant force. Nurturing the fact that, I could write...My words are not enough... But, all I say is that, 'Please, keep holding on to me...' u.d

My heartful thanks to Sujay Pusadkar for lending a creative hand and modeling this awe-inspiring cover page! And the patience that you kept with me all the way through...

My anchor in times of breaking down... Anshu, you know what you are to me.

My family for bearing with me...

Without whom this would have never been Possible

Gullybaba Publishers, it was such a pleasure working with this whole team, felt like home indeed. Thank you so much for being available for me even out of duty hours.

Mr. Dinesh Verma, can't thank you enough, for keeping me cool even in times of stress. You are an awesome personality to collaborate with.

I am thankful to the entire team of Gullybaba for helping me to complete this mountain-like task. You people have been a darling throughout.

I would love to work with you time and again...

The creative team was a fantastic experience to work with...

Born with a silver spoon in my mouth...

Dad was the world to me. For him, I was his
little angel, to grow to be.

Till, one day, all crumbled down. Suddenly,
I was a small adult.

*'Those Golden years
with Immortal relations,*

*How I wish you could've
taken me with you...*

*But, I guess, I'm left to taste
the changing times and HEARTS'...*

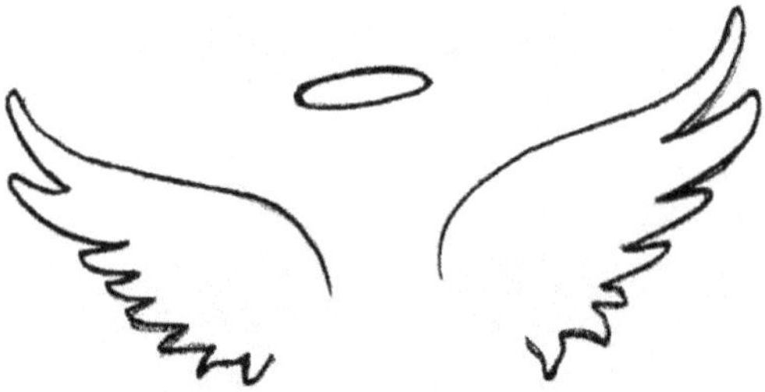

That unfaithful day, 17th March 1993...

Dad was one of the finest human beings that had ever set foot on this Earth. No, I'm not saying that coz he's my dad, but, that's what he was exactly as a being...The finest example of humanity, kindness, forgiveness, fitness, good deeds and my list can just go on and on...

I wish you never had set foot into that washroom, from, where you never ever returned back, but, ironically I'm so happy that it was so peaceful, so calm, so serene.

*'Isn't that the way Angels return
back to Heaven'.*

Me: *'Pa, why don't you ever go by a
rickshaw?'*

Dad: *'Let me walk the road till I AM.'*

Let that be my 'LAST WALK'...

(And Pa stuck to his words ...)

I was growing with the burden of being that
small adult.

How I was thrown into that dark, dark world of
wolves.

And, mom stood by like that wounded tigress to
help me through...

But, to nurture me to grow to be a fine human
being made her pay a lot at the hands of her
own relations and even her own children did
not spare her from the misery.

What was her mistake?

*Was this the cost mom had to pay being a
widow in our culture?*

Conditions were laid by my elder siblings
to mom,

*'Either you depart with your money and
property so that, we look after you and
your daughter or keep all, but, be
abandoned by us!'*

And there my journey also began...
I was never ever welcomed,
How, I was shoved away,
labelled as an orphan, but,
that didn't stop me...

Hey!! You people out there,
You all actually, made me stronger
and I took all your mockings as
challenges in time...

The television series 'Emergency' fascinated
me as a child and I was inspired by the
character Dr. Genen...

Always wanted to be like him, a doctor,
on a continuous run and a savior...

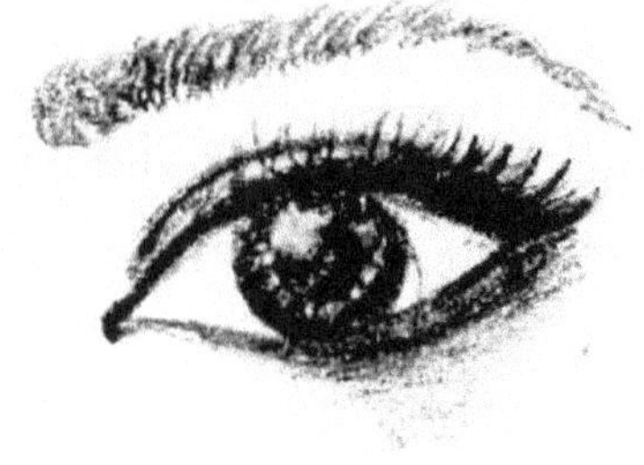

Dad had taken a promise from mom, what may
come, there should be no hindrances to me in
fulfilling my dream...

There, mom stood ALONE with his promise,
in a dilemma...

First, how to live her life all alone in a land that
was so alien to her...

Second, guide me, help me, protect me...

Without our guardian angel, taken
a heavenly abode...

How was she going to stand by me to fulfill
my ambition of being a doctor...

She also didn't know ...

All I could see was ....

Though, she was trying to smile again...

Those dark black eyes,

Didn't gleam, didn't shine

No more, no ways ...

And my quest began…

My journey to a foreign land. I didn't know where I was heading too. So naive, so ignorant.

Dad's last hug, still keeps me warm. That was the first time, I hugged him tight and cried on his shoulder. What I knew, those cries, were actually a departure to this beautiful being...MY DAD. Never ever to see him again. I sense him in all ways, everyday, in everything I do.

His last words to my friends...

*'She's very impulsive and loud but, mind
you, her heart is pure and soft…'*

He had actually fought our society to let me
fulfill my dream, 'A doctor should I be.'

Even his own siblings, just as mine, did not
spare him from their wrath of going against the
culture, where, the birth of a girl was mourned.
She was meant to look after her house, cook
and keep her husband happy. Forget going to
a foreign land and the least you could ask for,
was, being a doctor.

He always said...

'My child will never ever deceive my faith and
shall return back, being, what she always
wanted to be...'

Till date, these words ring in my ears, like the
daily chanting bells.

But, he also said...

*'My child, if, you don't like the place,
please, don't fear. You can return to your
place, that's HOME ...'*

But, in no way, was there a journey
backwards for me.

I was not a coward, to, let, the fears
overcome me!

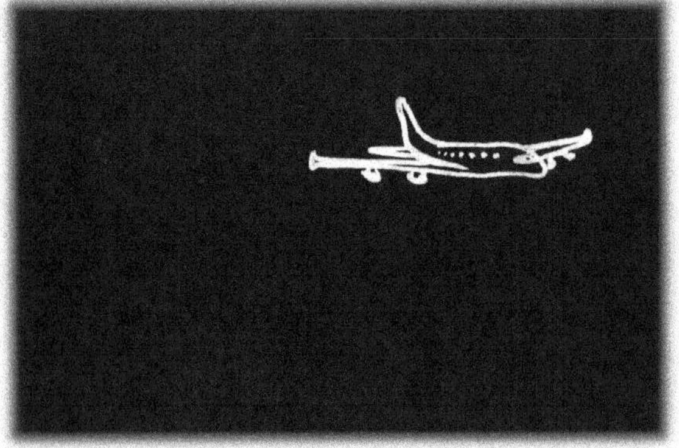

And there I was on my first solo flight sitting
next to a stranger.

The watch would just refuse to tick. A journey
of about four hours, was, as if, it's going
to be forever in the skies above...

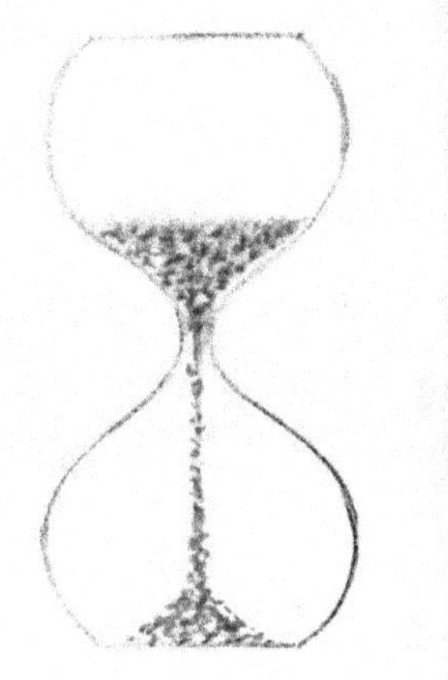

It was unexpectedly a warm welcome at the airport.

I was received by the Dean of my Medical Institute.

He was an absolute gentleman in his early 50's.

So kind and helpful, as, he could be, he was Mr. Mikhaelovich.

I was introduced to the other fellow students from different parts of the world. They would be studying with me at the same institution for almost seven years.

Oh! Boy...That's an awfully long time.

How would I get through?

My institute was around eight hours from the
capital by train, so, here, I go again...

My first ever journey on a train...

Lol, this train was an absolute synonym
of an aeroplane.

Beautiful it was, so comfortable, so smooth
as it could be.

I had a peaceful sleep in my compartment.
I was so tired and kind of scared too. But, that
didn't stop me from dozing off in this
ambience of serenity...

And at the crack of dawn, I peeped through my
compartment window. Crystal clear skies with a
hue of divine blue, so soothing
to my perplexed eyes!

I awaited my destination, a bit excited, a bit
jittery, a bit lonely. Wacky, weird thoughts gave
me goose bumps off and on.

But, I was excited too, embarking this
adventurous journey. I was a step closer
to fulfilling my life-long dream.

Thank you GOD!

Thank you Dad! Thank you Mom!

For all you have done for me ...

AMEN

The beautiful September breezes welcomed
me. It appeared to be a pleasant, small city.
But, being cautious,

I told to myself, 'Hey! Don't jump to any
conclusions!'

Mr. Mikhaelovich drove us past the city to our
hostel bypassing this city's landmark, an
enchanting church, 'Sabor'
that's what it was called.

'Little did I ever imagine that,
time and again

this Divine Harbor would be
my savior and only anchor...'

Roads were wide and all was so quite, maybe,
because it was the break of dawn.

Somehow, I was always at peace with the dark
or say just the break of dawn. At this point
of time, I could hardly differentiate between
the two, to believe in the dark
or the break of dawn.

42

Spooky it was...

As, Mr. Mikhaelovich pointed to our hostel.

He said, 'There it is, from the end of the road,
just prior to the approach, your's is hostel No. 4
and there are hostel No.s '1, 2 and 3.'

Oh GOD!! I wanted to run back HOME. It was
so dark, so lonely…. and I was so far,
far away…

There was an alley of steps leading to the hostel. It was a beautiful place though. It gave me a sense of security. I could feel that, I could call this my HOME, at least for the years to come...

The door to the entrance was a swinging wooden one.

Me and my colleagues (that's what I was beginning to recognize them as), along with Mr. Mikhaelovich entered. We were greeted by this smiling elderly lady at the reception, who greeted us with that shining smile and said, 'I'm Babulya.' I wondered, 'What's that now, maybe, that's her name!' But, later I learnt it's the native word for 'loving grandmother.'

And she made my journey over those years so safe, so pleasant. Thank you so much Babulya for that beautiful stay...

The waiting hall just on entering the hostel,
were those years of gatherings.

All those dance parties on New Year's Eve
every year, each year.

And mom praying back home for my safety and
a peaceful New Year to usher in and GOD help
me to be more closer to my dream coz she was
actually counting her days to be connected to
the heavens above...

Parties and gatherings continued... and so did
many beautiful memories.

I had to dwell in and I loved to socialize.
But, somehow because of being responsible for
any of my actions and the sacrifices of mom,
I always tried keeping a low profile.

For which, I was labelled as being reserved,
an arrogant snob by none other but, your own
nationals, who you thought would understand in
those difficult times to BE...

51

'Don't give me false hopes...

False wishes...

Please, don't give them to me

With that black heart of yours...

Don't need any...

I can survive, you, just don't worry'...

My hostel, Hostel No. 4, that's what it was called, a twelve storey coeducational nothing short from a five star lodge.

I was led by the hostel warden to my two-seater room on the ground floor to the right of the reception.

It was strange, why, a couple of senior students were making a runaway from the corridor of so to be called my room. I could see the smile with a tinge of sarcasm on their faces. Confused that's what I was!

Wasn't this whole journey a risk, what more I had to lose?

So, my mind started to rattle to explore this SECRET too...

The corridor led into 4 rooms where, there, were two 3-seater rooms and two 2-seater rooms. So these rooms would share a common kitchen (Just in case, as we were assigned specific meals at special canteens called Proflaktories, as per body mass index to regulate the calories intake, to keep us fit in body, mind and soul throughout, wasn't that just amazing!), common washroom and a common bath. All to be kept neat and clean by the allottees of this corridor.

A timetable hung on the corridor door showing the cleaning shifts with days and turns. Laundry was also to be done by oneself.

Oh LORD!! How would I handle all this!

But, gradually I learnt that it was an awesome technique to make oneself independent, meticulously organized and it was a mind blowing game of time management.

My room was just in front of the door that led
to this corridor. Room No. 103.

It was a beautiful, two-seater spacious room,
though it lay bare with a beautiful peachy
curtain hiding a big window behind...

As, I moved away that curtain...

The view SPOOKED me off the floor...

There stood a graveyard with tombstones...

This hostel was built on a pre-existing graveyard.

That's what I was told and part of the graveyard continued to the left of the building though this graveyard was beautifully maintained with flowers blooming all around.

As the years flew by...

This view was the only SOLACE to my
wandering thoughts and mind...

I could actually speak to THEM and somehow
get PEACE of my mind.

After all...

Don't we all end up there...

Isn't that the TRUTH of every life?

That cannot be escaped...

First day at the Medical Institution on the 1st of September (That's when the new educational year began) was very interesting.

The Institute Campus...

'What a beauty it was!'

Though, there were many adjacent buildings with the various departments.

But, the main building was a 'stargazer!'

It was a five storey building with the administrative block on the first floor.

The front side faced the main highway with the trams running across too.

The backyard was a beautiful garden, where, we could enjoy the serenity of those green, green trees, blooming flowers. And I just couldn't wait for those color changing falling leaves...

I believed it snowed here too, what a view with all laden in a carpet of pure white!

Mr. Mikhaelovich introduced us to Ms. Natalia.
She would be our future coordinator and
caretaker till time we were on the premises
of this country.

Ms. Natalia, a tall, elegantly built lady with dark
brown beautiful wavy hair flowing all the way
to her shoulders.

Her attire and those dark brown eyes were
something I adore till date.

She was just so amazing a person that all those
years

I saw her always smiling and that's what kept
me going...

Ms. Natalia... I thank you for being that, 'Ray of
Hope' for that dark tunnel that I didn't know was
leading me to where...

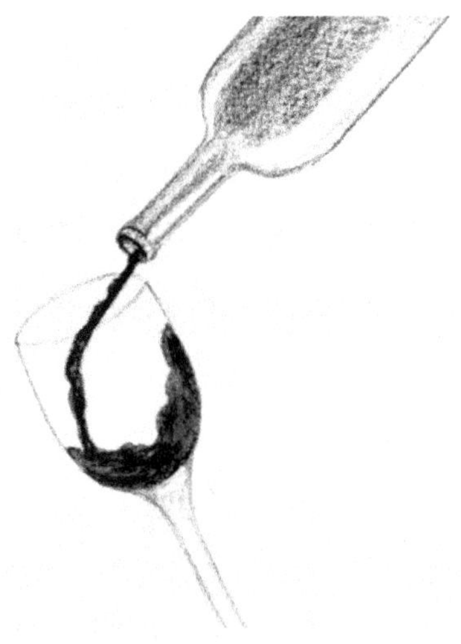

Ms. Natalia introduced us to the Rector
of the institute.

Mr. Kozlov, a generous, aged man with
a heart of gold.

So down to earth, no airs of his cadre. He even
travelled with us in the trams, you see...

He invited the fresher's batch over for dinner &
drinks.

That was a ritual that he followed year after
year since the time he was the Rector and
I heard it was since pretty long.

It was a beautiful small place with two
warm rooms.

But, I could sense what HOME could be...

Mr. Kozlov was a 'Father Figure' to me. You
could just walk up to him anytime, any place,
any day and give a piece of your
heart out to him.

That's what he was to me...

But, life has not been fair to everyone...

Destiny snatched Mr. Kozlov away. Don't beautiful souls leave early, ALWAYS?

He lost his battle to lung cancer. But, the only thing that quietened me from devastation was that,

'He died in PEACE.'

GOD rest his soul in peace FOREVER. Angels don't die, they guide you in every path you follow...

Classes were fun. Lectures were in very big cinematic halls carrying 500-600 students per lecture from all over the world.

I felt nothing alien in being in this foreign land.

Slowly I started getting in pace with the life out there....

Actually, enjoying every moment, everyday. I started to look forward to each coming day with enthusiasm.

But, deep down I was guilty because mom
was all alone out there.

That was not the era of watsapp or video
chatting. So, I had to wait long hours, long days
to talk to her and receive those beautiful cards,
those beautiful long letters from her.

I still have them in a tiny box all treasured
immensely.

But, don't you think that's what love
is all about....

These tiny things that we share be it a simple
wish on a plain paper or even a small card.

I still am and will always be that person who
loves those old fashioned beautiful simple
wishes... Though, people think of me
the other way.

First year into the institute was all about general
science and getting acquainted with their
Native language, their culture and the beautiful
country.

Wasn't that an amazing way to get you
comfortable!

So practical, so patient that's what they were
with me...

Roopinder Dogra

A month in this beautiful land of ecstasy...

Days whisked running between the hostel and
the main building (that's where our classes
were for the first year).

And those nights of solace talking to those
tombstones peeping through my window...

This was my first telephonic talk with mom
since I reached here...

The receptionist came running knocking on my
door on that fine evening. She was so elated to
see my gleaming eyes and contagious smile,
dimpling my right cheek.

She said, 'Hey! You are so pretty indeed, why
don't you smile more often?'

That's when I looked into the mirror and
thought, 'Really?'

And ran to speak to mom

Mom tried her best to be confident and happy
as she spoke to me.

But, how could she fool a part of her's!!

Mom, 'I know you are dying inside. I can sense
that loneliness within.'

You don't need money, you don't need
servants, you just need that ONE to be by your
side to understand your mind and soul. That's
another kind of intimacy.

At that point of time, I was too young, too naive
to understand these intimate emotions, because
I had been brought up too protected, that,
I knew love is only dad and mom...

What exactly LOVE is all about, I have just
begun to understand only NOW...

Rest all was just a good understanding and
a compromise with the situations. A mere
adjustment under society pressures
to keep them happy!

So I tried following the hostel receptionist's
words.

Whenever, she saw me, she would point
out to smile...

But, deep within she, also knew, that, there was
a very dark secret hidden within me. Even
those expensive lipsticks could not hide
that fake smile...

Not forgetting that,

Those dark moments

Are lived all ALONE...

Roopinder Dogra

Then was the beautiful month of October. How,
I adore this month! My Birthday, the first fall and
how to forget Halloween...

I witnessed the first fall, how the leaves
withered, changing into a dazzling golden,
red, yellow and then drying off...

Doesn't this explain the cycle of our lives?

Roopinder Dogra

I waited for that last leaf on the bare tree to fall,
but, to my surprise, it clinged on and on...

I kept peeping at it, at every… break of dawn,
giving me signals that if, I can hold on,
so can you...

Roopinder Dogra

Birthday...

Has always been a very emotional day for me,
sad yet, happy reminiscing those beautiful
memories...

Dad used to specially come for my cake cutting
taking an hour's leave from his office...

And mom, busy in baking and cooking, all was
made at home so fresh and tasted so homely.

Maturity brings the essence of every moment, every relation…

That's what I've sensed with passing of time...

Days rolled by...

I made many new acquaintances but, still
shared all my moments in those quiescent dark
nights with those standing tombstones,
they were all that I had...

And there were the first snowflakes in the early
days of December.

Those powdery flakes, melting away on my
face, my hands. I thought it would be freezing
cold, but, it was so cool, a feel
of eternal PEACE...

All covered in white...

So, so pure, an absolute blissful sight!

Days whisked one by one and my night
conversations somehow shifted
to the shining moon.

I guess those tombstones had nothing
more to hear from me...

*I shared everything with
the moon...*

*And she promised that it's just
going to be between
Her and Me...*

Not even the stars...

So I waited eagerly for each night to talk with her.

The day, she was not meant to be, I put myself somehow to sleep, pacifying myself that she would talk more the following night...

Blended into a lot of customs
and cultures...

Christmas being celebrated
on the 7th of January.

All covered in white, waiting for Santa
Claus to arrive on his red reindeer
driven sledge. Tall, beautifully
decorated Christmas trees stood in
every house, every shop. A scintillating
moment indeed...

Women's Day, 8th March made me feel
so so special.

Really appreciated their respect and
love, how gifts, roses and cakes were
exchanged! It was all so exciting.

And lol! It was a holiday. How, I waited
for this day each year, every year.

Year-end exams finally finished in June.

The days were amazingly long till 23:00hrs.
So, my conversations with the moon somehow
shortened and the days started to keep me
warm.

Everyone was happy to return home for their
three months' long term holidays to start a fresh
new year in September.

Where did I stand at this point of time?

I really didn't know where I was headed to. This was my first visit back to mom in the dead silence of the grieves.

I actually never ever stayed at that place. It was a small city but, well developed and densely populated. The house was nothing more than a guesthouse to me. I was heading there just for mom.

Mom refused to let go of that house.

Who was I to pluck her away from those cherished memories?

At that point of time, that, was all I could give her, 'Let her be at peace in that place.' She could actually see dad, that's what she shared with me ...

And I shared it with the moon ...

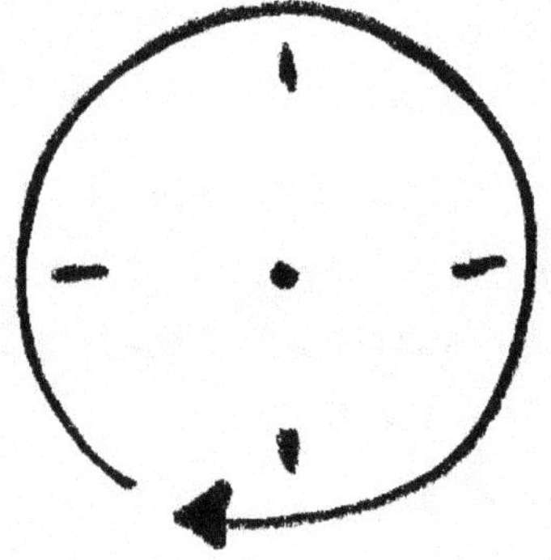

I could never call this mansion of a place
as HOME.

The place was so raw, still under renovation
and dad suddenly left ...

It was here that destiny snatched him away
from us, so untimely…

Suitcases and all utilities still lay unpacked and
everything lay as it was!

Everyone had moved ON, but, mom just stayed
frozen in time ...

I stood there at the gate of the house. All seemed so hollow, so EMPTY...

The iron gate was locked from inside, showing mom's sense of being insecure.

I rang the bell. It took her a while to ajar that gate.

I could see her struggling to do it, but, she was always graceful in whatever she did...

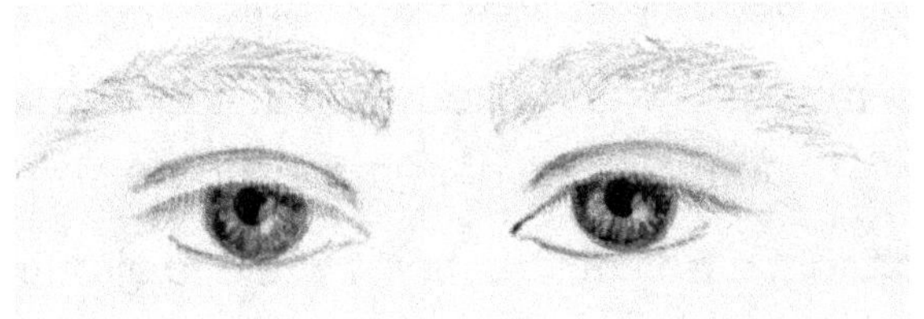

Mom was an epitome of beauty. I'm not saying this because she was my mom. She was so natural, so pleasant, so feminine...

She hugged me tight. I dare not let her cry!

But, her hug was cold. I could sense her brokenness within.

Dad, how I missed your warm hug! Could you give me your shoulder just one more time to cry on?

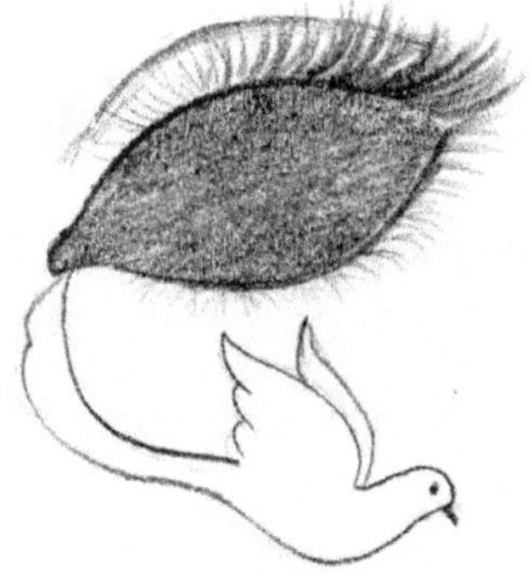

She looked at me with that fake beautiful smile.
Her translucent peachy skin shined against the
rays of the sun. I loved her lovely jet black long
wavy hair.

Her dark black eyes were so empty, so dry,
as if, there were no more tears to cry...

And I asked, 'Mom, what's for lunch?

I'm so hungry.'

And she replied, 'Your favorite, Kadi Chawal.'

'I wish your dad was here to make it the way
you liked it!'

And we both broke down...

Hugged each other so tight and I felt a warmer hug from above...

Yeah, I could sense. Dad, 'I know you are here'...

The house was a huge two-storey mansion with around 10 rooms. Voices echoed as we spoke.

Days were spent basking in the sun. Pulling mom out to the market as, she never wanted to step out!

But, those nights were rather spooky.

I could hear the owls hooting and there were even bats flying around.

There was a railway track just behind this house. The running of these trains could wake up the dead in that dark silence.

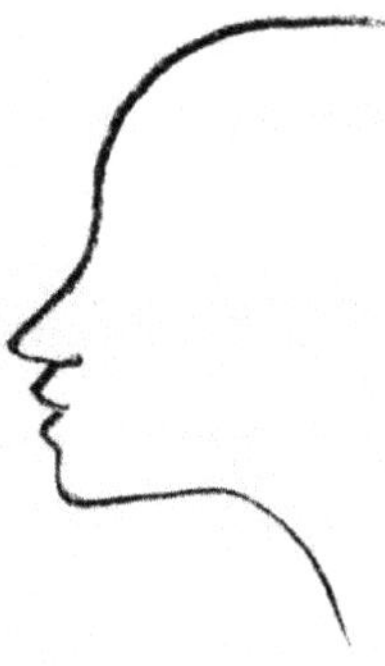

I wondered how mom stayed all alone in this mansion.

There were helpers who would do their chores in the daytime and leave by evening.

I persuaded her to come along with me, since, seven years would be a long time. But, she said, 'I'm not alone, your dad is with me!'

There was no way I could break her belief. So I thought of taking one step at a time.

Mom was still in a state of shock and I was hoping that time would heal...

But, am I ever able to get over this till today? Then, how could she...

Over the days of my stay, I noticed we had no visitors and no house to visit to either. Except, my uncle's place (My dad's eldest brother). He was very elderly about 85 years of age staying with his only son, daughter-in-law and four grandchildren (two boys and two girls).

We used to get along very well and they used to be frequent rendezvous when dad was there. So, what's the reason of this coldness, I wondered ...

One fine day, I picked up the courage and asked mom, 'Why don't they come over anymore or we visit them?'

Mom after much hesitation answered, 'It's a tough culture out here, you will understand over the years as you mature'...

I gazed at her blankly and could not understand what she meant!

All I could understand was that, if, you're
a widow, it's all your fault, so somehow
the society abandons you.

Why did she not have an equal right to
live the way she wanted? I even felt that
the breaths that she took were
with permission!

It was nerve-wracking to see her
breaking within day after day... Was this
society ever going to be happy if she
lived their way, so why not GO YOUR's
was my question to her
and she just smiled ...

And all I could do was just watch her.
But, I assured her, that, I'll be by her side
till the end of time what may come and
I tried to keep that promise...

It's tough when your own siblings
instead of thanking relatives for helping
mom out start placing allegations
on them.

Now, this was a new twist to the whole
situation, which, was spilled to me by
our family physician (he was a well
qualified cardiologist), Dr. Sethi.

Mom was a constant guest at their place
and was very friendly with his mother.
A very decent, down to earth family.

I thank this family from the core of my
heart for keeping mommy going…

Dr. Sethi was a very great stepping force
in my life and guided me through the
seven years of my medical training.

It was time to get back. A whole new year.
I was stepping into my second year of
medicine.

I promised mom to be in constant touch and my
target being the foremost goal of my life.

She tried to smile, standing there, at the gate of
the house and I dared not to look back...

I knew she was not alone, dad was by her side
and that's why somehow that house kept her
SECURE...

Years rolled by…

Studies got tougher. I had classes and lectures
in various setups, far, far away from my hostel.

Had to get up really early to make it to the tram
stop, else, I would have to wait for another
hour, if, I missed that one…

Latecomers were forbidden entry into the
lecture halls and the practical premises and
I couldn't afford to miss any of these as I learnt,

'Medicine is no excuse of,
I didn't learn that!'

Snowfalls were fun, but, not when you found yourself embedded into the snow upto your knees, that's when your hurrying was slowed down so awfully...

Some days were freezing cold with the temperature dropping to minus degrees.

Summers were warm though but, just the months of June and July, that's why no infrastructure had any ceiling fans at all!

But, in spite of all this, I loved their organized lifestyle, which, taught me punctuality and the most important concept of prioritizing.

I mastered the art of time management although my dad had taught me that pretty well since I was 5 years of age...

Some subjects and lecturers were really tough going (Histology, Pathology, Pathological physiology, Paediatric Diseases), but, that didn't break my courage or interest.

I just kept going on...

And I guess my conversations with the moon, night, after night, helped me to pull through. There was an aura of positivity around her!

WITH
LOVE

Mom's letters kept coming through every 2-3 months.

She never forgot to send me my Birthday Card with wishes. Christmas and New Year was my favorite season.

So, it was always a huge card with her beautiful hand written wishes on it, she drew too artistically as well.

But, I could sense that loneliness in her. Her handwriting had begun to change. There was a trembling stroke to it. That's when I realized things are not going right.

My visits to mom continued every year from mid June till the last week of August. She refused to come with me, in spite of, persistent insistence.

She said, 'I'm waiting here for you.'

'I've promised your dad this, till you get through'….

She tried to stay steady, but, was breaking bit by bit within...

By that time...

I was already into my fifth year of medicine.

I had to get into the core of the matter,

Something was being kept aloof from me...

That June, as I visited mom...

She opened the gate as every year, but,
this time it was different...

She stood there in all WHITE, shriveled
and broken!

I asked her, 'What the hell is this now?'

She replied, 'This's my attire now!'

'What bullshit!' I thought...

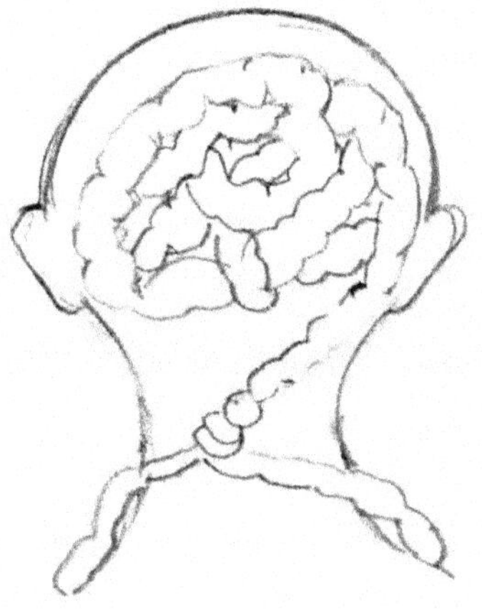

It was so sad, how the pressures of the society
had totally downtrodden mom...

Even her children stopped visiting her!

What a wonderful world this is, with black
hearts and white blood!

I just ask you all,

'Where are you all running too?'

'For work, for Money'...

'You forget your priorities!'

What's more precious than mom...?

Her shuffling gait had begun to disturb me. Her
hands had started trembling, speech slurred...

This was not the strong, self-confident lady that
I knew...

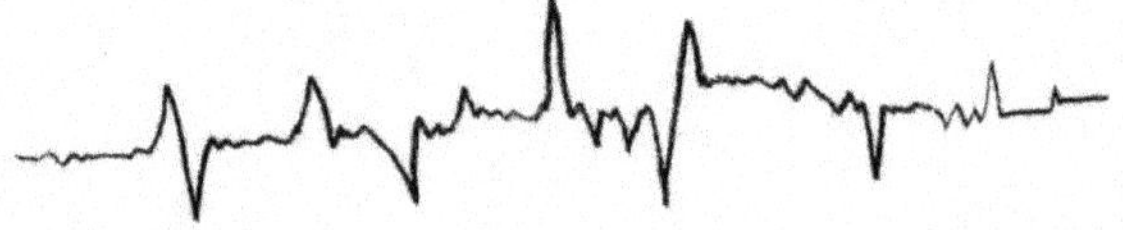

After meeting her, I straight away
headed to Dr. Sethi.

He was the only one who could let me know,
what, exactly was going on...

He revealed certain heart breaking facts to me,
saying, hope I could understand him at such
a young age...

Circumstances mature you, really really fast.
Don't they?

Mom was suffering from depression. An aftermath of severe emotional blows too fast in time.

Especially, when you are discarded by the ones who were your own, a part of you... Your children! What more heartbreaking can anything else BE....

Abandoned, no one to converse with, elements of dementia too set in.

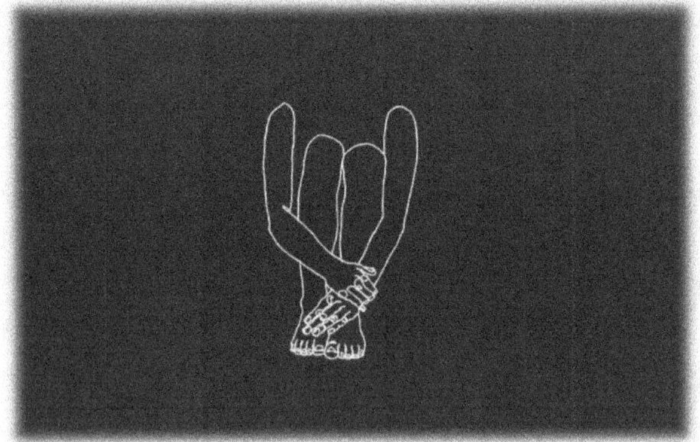

I asked Dr. Sethi, 'Why?'

And he replied, 'It's sad, when your own children raise fingers at your character and you've to prove to them your innocence!'

What was all this going on?

'Yes!' He replied, unfortunately this was true.

So, mom stopped visiting relatives and friends...

Except, Dr. Sethi's mother and another very close elderly aunt of mine who stayed close by. This aunty knew mom like an open book. I'm in touch with her till date...

Why can't mom live on her own terms and conditions?

What was she being punished for!

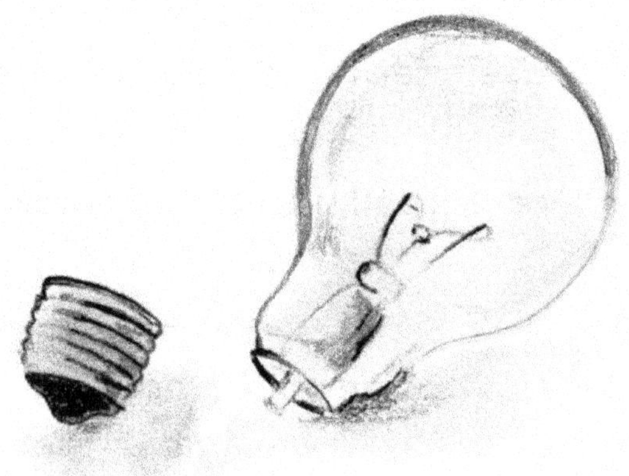

Her tremors and jerky movements were due to some elements of early Parkonism.

Unfortunately, all set in very early for her because of mental pressures from society, from her own children leading her to the verge of conscience guilt.

Certain phone calls were disturbing her.
That's why

I was forbidden from taking any of the calls...

But WHY?

So one day, without mom's knowledge as
I picked up this call, to my bewilderment, these
were actually hoax, threatening calls, to leave
the house, or they could get me raped and
murdered!!!

Height of cheapness...

I wondered, wasn't this house ours, so why
were we asked to leave...

And it was none other than mom's sisters,
eyeing the property and money. Even, her own
father didn't spare her from a deal...

I wasn't going to sit around like a coward
or a sheep.

Got a police complaint lodged and
phone tapped. I thought it my moral duty
to inform my elder brothers about the
incident to guide what else could be
done.

But, it really shocked me, when I was
replied as,

'Why don't you get the telephone
disconnected?'

'Simple as that, all problems solved'...

But, was I going to do that, how could
mom connect in any times of need!!

Finally, after a few days, those calls
suddenly stopped...

BUT !!

In the midst of those silent dark nights,
someone started to bang on the main gate,
every night...

I was not afraid to run out and see, but, mom
made me swear on her, that, I will not…

So, I started keeping a knife under my pillow as
I slept during those dreadful nights, just in
case...

And of course praying and I knew all would be
fine, with dad around and the moon sheltering!!

It was time to get back, September already
rolled in and I was now into my sixth year.

How I persuaded mom to come along with me,
but, as always, she smiled and said, 'Come
fast... Your dad is waiting for me, I've promised
him to be here only, till you finish your
medicine!'

And with a heavy heart I had to leave her again,
yet, for another year...

174

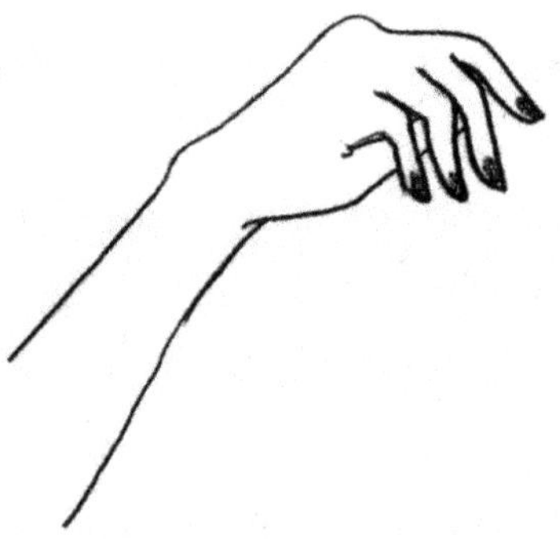

Multiple problems cropped up in those years,
which were not dealt with…

This left mom dejected, hopelessly alone
leaving her depressed and being all isolated...

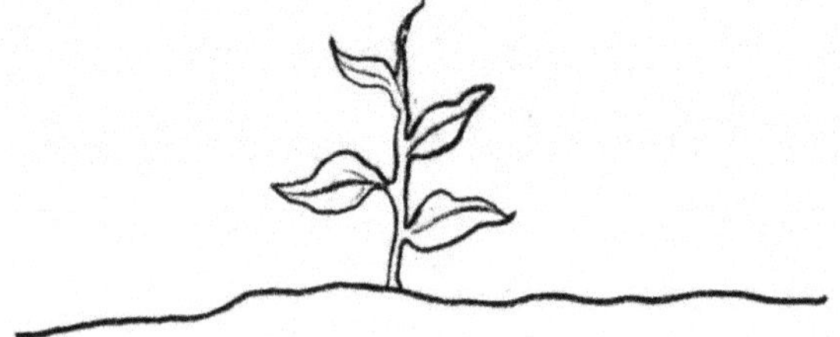

The last two years were, entirely, practically oriented. I had many night shifts along with the morning college.

This was a technique of training to be alert in the forthcoming night duties, once, I start working as a professional.

It was in this sixth year, that, I met that
person who actually brought a major
twist in my career, Ms. Vera Nikolaevna.

An enchanting personality, a tall blonde
lady with a thin, lean structure. Oh Gosh!
She looked like a ramp model! She was
my Obstetrics & Gynaecology teacher.
We jelled marvelously because her
daughter was in the same batch as mine.

I became a regular invitee at her house
and loved those americanos with vanilla
ice cream. That's from where
I developed a craving for dark coffee,
dark chocolate and their local vanilla ice
creams were just out of the blue.

The local cake was in the shape of a train
called 'Skaska' meaning fairytale and
indeed that cake tasted like Heavenly
Earth, I have never tasted anything like
that ever again...

180

Ms. Nikolaevna, trained me so well practically as well as theoretically, that, this became my favorite subject.

I usually used to do night shifts with her.

That's how I decided, I would take up Obstetrics & Gynaecology as my future specialization.

*'It was so beautiful to see a new life
coming into being*

It was a science of happiness and bliss…

A ray of sunshine

Deafening away the darkness

I had been in for so so long'…

Mom's letters stopped coming suddenly...

Telephonic calls were difficult because the network was usually busy or bad. Even, if connected, were received after various rings in view of her increasing shuffling gait and tremors that made it difficult for her to pick up the receiver.

Her slurred speech had increased. It was getting difficult for her to hold a pen to write. Her vision was also getting weak, although, she was just 50 years of age in all!

How circumstances and culture liabilities take a toll on you!!

Oh GOD! Please bless her and help me. I have just the last year to go, that's what I always prayed for and the Moon smiled back...

Don't worry...

I'm looking on her

Don't you worry, but, just hurry...

184

I really want to name a very dear friend,
Neelika she's from Sri Lanka.

I found SOLACE in her. She had that level of
maturity to understand the turmoil within me.

Although, during those days, due to some petty
misunderstandings, we parted ways to meet
again last year...

This was my last summer before I returned finally back to mom.

So, this time, in spite of visiting her, I was actually not being with her. I had to complete my practical trainings under various setups as my practical homework.

How heart breaking, when, your own siblings commented, 'Why does she come down every year, Isn't it a waste of money, especially, when dad is not there anymore?'

How would these white blooded people know, money can be earned, but, a life lost, shall never ever return…

All those years, I was just coming down for mom …

I too wanted to enjoy hiking, summer camping,
mountain climbing, trips to other countries and
cities like my colleagues.

But, I didn't give my mind the permission to
enjoy or my heart to love...

All I knew was that, I had to study hard, reach
my target and get back to mom...

Dr. Sethi asked me, 'Do you know, how your mom has been getting through all these years?'

I looked at him perplexed, 'How?'

'What do you mean?'

He replied, 'let me explain... January to June she's busy making preparations that you are coming. June to August it's all listening to your nonstop talks (Omg! I've always been a chatterbox). September to December, remembering your talks and waiting for January to start the preparations afresh'...

These words till date ring in my head. How destiny plays it's game...

Into my last (seventh) year, I left, promising
mom that I would be back soon this time for
good...

And she promised to take good care of herself.

Days whisked by so soon...

I was being offered a scholarship for my
specialization in Obstetrics & Gynaecology at
the same institute, but, how could I join, mom
refused to come along and it was no way, this
time I was going to let her stay back alone...

I could not be so selfish. It's time, she needs me.

I told Ms. Nikolaevna, 'I'm so sorry, but,
I cannot accept because I got to get back, I've
responsibilities'...

She asked, 'What will you do there?'

'You have never stayed there!'

And I replied,

GOD is great!

*HE will find a way for me there or
somewhere...*

194

Final exams were just round the corner...

There I was sitting in front of the photographer in a studio getting clicked for my graduation degree.

By Joe! Seven years have whisked away, it's just like it was yesterday, when I was at the same studio being clicked by the same photographer for my student's card.

My eyes turned moist and he thought they were sparkling in the photograph that he had clicked...

Exams went really well…

Finally, it was Graduation Day. I was asked to dress up in my National Costume.

Oops!! How was I gonna wear... Never been in one before. That was the first and last time I adorned it. I decided to flaunt my favorite orange color!

It was a beautiful Graduation ceremony all were in black robes and caps so elegantly. The evening dinner was so relishing, I loved all their delicacies. The salads, soups, cakes and that local ice cream. How I was gonna miss all these. Those last moments were rather too emotional....

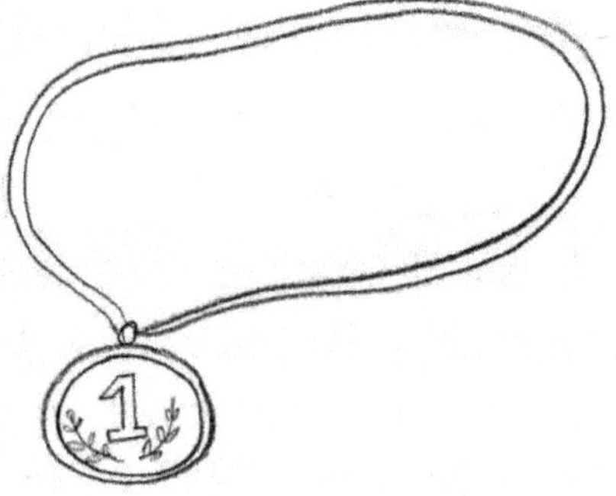

At the ceremony, I suddenly heard
a name being announced...

I was flabbergasted, Oh Boy! That's
mine...

I was awarded the 'Most Outstanding
Foreign Student' award. I completed my
graduation in Honors with a Red Medal!
This was an absolute surprise...

First thing, that came into my mind....
'How was I going to get to that stage in
this costume!! Leave alone what I was
going to speak!'

I had to walk to it and before reaching
to the podium had to climb a couple of
stairs. 'What if I tripped off, what if the
costume fell off, yicks!!!!

But, the audience would just not let me
be... They begun to call out my name
and clap…

Lol! I was standing behind the lectern...

'I have no papers to read from. No preparations at all', that's how I started after greeting my teachers, colleagues and friends...

'How all these years just flew away?
But, I tend to stay at that very place
At that, very moment in time have influenced'...

And I continued...

'Thank you ALMIGHTY,

Thank you dad, thank you mom for letting me be in such a beautiful country with such lovely people'...

'This has been and will always
Be the most cherishing years of my life
Although, there was darkness all around
But, I was enlightened with that hope
And I would not be justified in naming a few

Each one of you has influenced me in
someway somehow sometime
somewhere'...

And In my hearts of heart... How could
I forget those tombstones peeping
through my window and the moon
smiled over me as she would go
wherever I would be...

There was no end to those claps; I just
had to move away now else I would
break down…

This was the best piece of the student's
heart they had ever heard that's what
was conveyed to me!

The Graduation ceremony had a grandeur
giving away of our certificates and we pledged
on the OATH to be truthful in our services.

That's when I saw a glimpse of a shadow just
next to me and felt a warm hand over my head.
As, I turned to see there was nothing, no one,
but,
I knew it was DAD...

Time to pack my bags and head back to mom...

Mixed feelings, words are falling short
to express...

All I can say that it was the same agonizing pain
that I experienced seven years ago, but, this
time more stronger, more confusing. How,
I loved this place, how I wished mom had
agreed to come along and life would've been
so beautiful, so serene, so calm...

I could sense I was entering into an
unprecedented world out there!

But, I was just happy where she was happy,
at least she would not be alone...

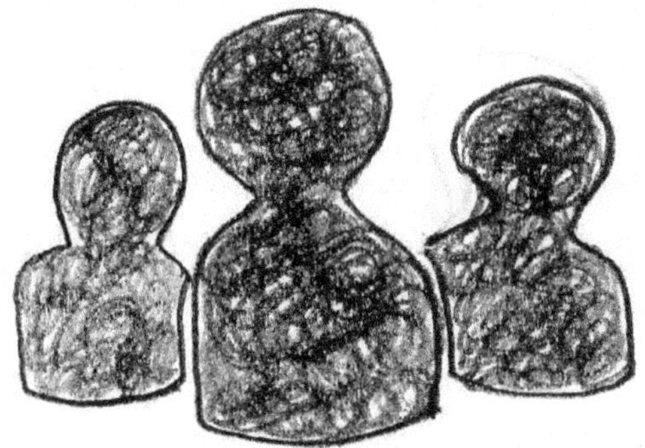

So, there I was standing once again at the gate of that house...

This time it was different, the gate was opened by mom's youngest sister! I was confused, but, maybe happy, I thought relations had mended.

But, it was proved once again, money makes blood white, whose ever it is!

I was so excited to show my graduation degree to mom.

But, as I showed it to her, I realized, she was sitting there just as a corpse!

Her three sisters with their husbands had been coming often in this last year, as they, knew it was time for me to get back for good...

So, can you believe it!

They all coaxed her into giving away the house to them, for a petty amount of cash, making her believe that, since I was getting back, cash would be more important than a house!

How an emotionally broken person takes such vulnerable steps... Mom kept a belief in her sisters, thinking, they were doing right, who do you believe now?

So how did they manage to actually get to doing all this!

After much digging, I got to the core of it...

It was due to mom's persistently increasing tremors, that, she was unable to write distinctly. So, she actually stopped signing any legal documents. Wherever, necessary it was replaced by her thumb impression. I never knew this. This was disclosed by the Bank Manager to me!

So, these circumstances made it easier for them to take mom's thumb impression on an empty court paper and the contents were filled in later...

Believing them, she only realized now what she had done, but, it could not be undone as these people were very shrewd.

Mom always held herself responsible for this, but, I assured her, maybe, it's for our BEST...

I wanted to stay back and backlash ... How in the humanity's sake could anybody do a thing like that…

This was another challenge I had to face but, what would happen to all those sacrifices that dad and mom made to make me what I am, I thought...

A very tough decision it was because I couldn't be selfish all the time, just, thinking about me!

But, Dr. Sethi advised, 'These are very dangerous, ruthless people. Your medical degree is your asset. That's what your dad and mom had retaliated for, all along. Forget this Money and house! With your calibre and degree, you will earn a lot and foremost DIGNITY!

Please, take her, she's suffered too much and leave this place for good...

Your mom needs peace of mind, Else, these people will throw you both on the roads!'

Mom just refused to leave that house!

I assured her that we shall just shut it down for the time being and then I shall return back to sort it all out once we are safe in another city...

But, somehow, she didn't believe me or those memories were just holding her too tight...

Dr. Sethi decided to put her on antidepressants before we left that place because the depression was in a stage which now required some kind of a treatment, as, there would be a change of an environment.

But, one morning, while I was still asleep, mom, walked down to Dr. Sethi's residence and spoke to his mom.

She said, 'They all think I'm mad, see what they want to put me on!'

His mom tried to persuade mom, that, it's nothing like that, it's just for the time being...

But, mom refused relentlessly...

I was dead sure that we have to leave the house and the city to come back later...

I started to pack little by little over the days. I gave off a lot of stuff that was not required to the needy.

I decided to head to the capital. I thought that's the only place where I shall get ample opportunities and a good treatment for mom too. I had no acquaintances out there, but, we had to leave, that's all

I knew...

One of my medical institute's colleague was staying in the capital, so agreed, to help me get an apartment as a paying guest near to the hospital where, I could possibly apply for my internship.

I could see mom breaking even further. She held me the culprit for letting GO of dad's memories of that place.

She labelled me as being selfish, but, all said and done ...

'Mom in no way was I going to let you stay there, she refused to understand that the place was now under legal problems because of her sisters' capture of the house and the matter has to be resolved legally in the court of law. We could no longer stay in that place for long!'

I assured her that memories are not with a place, it's in our hearts.

'Memories don't depart, don't fade ...
We cherish them as long as we are ...

Dad's always with us, it's his decision actually, that's my belief...

It was Christmas Eve, foggy and rather cold...

I gave mom sleeping pills in her supper.

In the wee hours of the morning at around 3am, my cousin brother's sons came over to help us to LEAVE...

They helped to carry mom to the SUV cab as she was fast asleep...

I had nothing to carry from that place, except loads of memories, some photo albums, my study table and two chairs with it (This was dad's gift to me) two folding beds and two suit cases.

The gate was locked from the inside by my nephews, a corridor bulb was left to light, after which they jumped over the house's wall to get out!

These precautions were taken, so that, no one would suspect that mom & I, had actually left the place in the wee hours of the morning. As, per my promise to mom, I would definitely be returning back to settle this legal issue.

My ailing sleeping mom and I with this
unknown taxi driver were headed to the capital
and I realized it was Christmas Day,
my favorite season.

The moon still peeping above us blending with
the rays of the rising sun, it was the break of
dawn. What a coincidence, it was exactly the
same setup as I peeped through my train
compartment, seven years ago…

This was going to be a long 7-8 hours drive...

I was exhausted, though mentally. How,
I wanted a pillow to just let me sleep.

But... There was one last stop, before the
sun brightens the blue skies, wholly...

I was in search of an abandoned spot,
with lots of trees...

It had to be closer to the destination to
be...

Being vigilant, keeping a track of the distance covered with the help of milestones along the highway. I dare not share a single word!

Just then, we approached towards that perfect spot. I asked the driver to halt...

He was perplexed, rather scared. But, not more than me. My heart was thumping, lub dub, lub dub... I couldn't catch my breath, it was like my heart would jump out of my mouth...

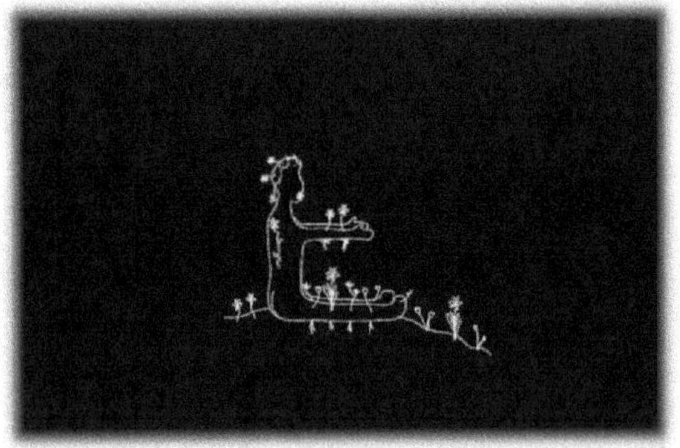

I told him...

'Please, give me five minutes
& I shall be back'...

He refused to stay alone with my
sleeping mom, thinking I would abandon
her and run away, as, he saw me taking
my purse along...

So, we struck upon a deal, that, he gets
to keep my wallet and jewelry as a
security.

But, how could I believe this man! What
if, he threw mom on the empty road &
just whisked off...

I was so scared. I had no choice, but,
to just pray...

Humanity does exist
This world is not all that

Full of betray...

That's when the moon peeped through the trees as if, giving an assurance, that, she would keep a watch till I returned...

I walked into this forest like area. In the dead of the night, I could hear my own footsteps, crushing against the grass beneath.

I had to be just a few feet in, not too deep and there the torch just refused to light!

It was a full moon night, so bright, that enabled me to accomplish my task effectively...

I took IT out from my purse!

I had found this back in the house's store room while packing.

Dad was fond of firearms. So, had purchased one, way way back... It was a licensed one.

I don't think, mom remembered about it.

It was a safety in disguise for all those years spent in that house ALONE, that's my belief…

I had decided to bury it, in an abandoned area, as, that's what would give me peace of mind…

Digging hurriedly with the spade that I had carried along, I dropped it into the pit, covering it, as, not to leave any trace, lest, anyone should be harmed.

I had actually broken it into pieces for security reasons way back in the store room!

All done, within five minutes, I was back into the car.

Oh GOD! I was sweating on that cold cold foggy night…

I thanked GOD to the moon and back...

I signaled the driver to start the car,
knowing that the dilemma would always
remain on his mind!

And there, a whole new adventure,
yet, again…

But, with a tremendous difference...

'Mom! You are with me!'

And not forgetting dad's memories with us...

(PEACE BE ALWAYS UPON HIM)

Roopinder Dogra

Divine Intervention

Just want to share...

All along my journey in writing this book,

a shooting star kept peeping through my
window, while writing, each night, every
night...

The night, I penned down the last page
of this book, the shooting star has not

peeped till date...

www.ingramcontent.com/pod-product-compliance
Lightning Source LLC
LaVergne TN
LVHW010021150726
843364LV00039B/1132